Columbia University

Contributions to Education

Teachers College Series

No. 63

AMS PRESS
NEW YORK

INDIVIDUAL DIFFERENCES IN ABILITY AND IMPROVEMENT AND THEIR CORRELATIONS

J. CROSBY CHAPMAN

B. A. (Camb.); D. Sc. (London)
Ph.D. (Columbia)

TEACHERS COLLEGE, COLUMBIA UNIVERSITY
CONTRIBUTIONS TO EDUCATION, No. 63

Published by
Teachers College, Columbia University
NEW YORK CITY
1914

Library of Congress Cataloging in Publication Data

Chapman, James Crosby, 1889-1925.
  Individual differences in ability and improvement
and their correlations.

  Reprint of the 1914 ed., issued in series: Teachers
College, Columbia University. Contributions to
education, no. 63.
  Orginially presented as the author's thesis, Columbia.
  Bibliography: p.
  1. Mental tests. 2. Variability (Psychometrics)
I. Title. II. Series: Columbia University. Teachers
College. Contributions to education, no. 63.
BF431.C4 1972   153.9'32   74-176636
ISBN 0-404-55063-0

Reprinted by Special Arrangement with Teachers
College Press, New York, New York

From the edition of 1914, New York
First AMS edition published in 1972
Manufactured in the United States

AMS PRESS, INC.
NEW YORK, N.Y.   10003

CONTENTS

ACKNOWLEDGMENTS

It is my pleasure to record my obligation to Professor E. L. Thorndike, not only for suggesting the subject and the plan of this research, but also for his help and ready advice throughout the work. I also wish to express my thanks to the New York State Ventilation Commission for their courtesy in permitting me to use these results for the present study.

J. C. C.

INDIVIDUAL DIFFERENCES IN ABILITY AND IMPROVEMENT AND THEIR CORRELATIONS

Introduction

The statistical side of this study has been undertaken with a view to obtaining evidence on some of the questions which are the most pressing in the subject of individual differences. It is obvious that the experimental determination of the efficiencies of the same individual in various tests is a problem of wide theoretical interest as well as of educational importance. This measurement of efficiencies has received considerable attention, but the lack of a definite answer to such a fundamental question as the following, indicates the large field of investigation which is still open. This question in its broadest aspect may be stated. Is there any such thing in mental achievement as general improvability ? Does it follow that the individual who gains rapidly in one measured trait will also gain with corresponding rapidity in all similar traits'? Only from a very limited study of Wimms ('07) can any answer to this question be given. It is one of the objects of this study to throw light on this problem of general improvability.

The scope of the paper is indicated by the range of subjects which will be investigated in the following order:

1. The nature of composite and practise curves.
2. The correlation between initial abilities in various functions.
3. The correlation between initial and final abilities in various functions.
4. The correlation between improvability in one function and improvability in other functions.
5. The correlation between initial ability and improvability in each function.
6. The correlation between efficiency and accuracy in each function.

A considerable amount of work has already been published dealing with the effects of practise on a wide range of activities, for in no case has practise over a sufficiently long period failed to produce an appreciable amount of improvement: to this extent this research will merely supplement the previous information.

The results on correlation will be of greater interest, for not only are the present determinations comparatively few, but hitherto owing to the conditions under which the experiments have been performed, from the results stated it is impossible to make any investigation of the correlation between improvabilities in the tests employed.

The method of procedure adopted throughout this research enables a tentative answer to be given concerning many of the questions which involve this factor of improvability; it also leads to an important conclusion concerning the use of improvement as a measure of individual differences.

Twenty-two individuals have been examined in tests varying from color naming to somewhat difficult mental multiplication. In each case the experiment was sufficiently extended to allow a considerable amount of improvement, so that not only have we the initial scores in each one of the tests from which the usual correlations of static efficiencies can be calculated but we are also provided with a knowledge of the improvability of each individual in each function; thus enabling conclusions to be drawn concerning the more interesting dynamic problem of the correlation between improvabilities in the various mental tests. From the educational standpoint, it is certainly of great interest that taking a particular group at a particular time we should know what is the likely correlation between their efficiencies at that time, but it is of even greater importance that correlations between improvabilities should if feasible be determined. As education is always interested in the dynamic side, the significance of powers of improvement as opposed to mere static efficiency is obvious.

General Conditions of Experiment

The data used in connection with this research were obtained during investigations made upon subjects selected by the New York State Ventilation Commission for the purpose of investigating the psychological and physiological effects of various external physical conditions of temperature and humidity. The primary purpose of the tests therefore was to measure not so much individual differences as to discover the effects on mental efficiency of these external conditions of ventilation. As explained later it is permissible to neglect the differences in conditions so as to use these same results for the study of individual differences. In considering the methods adopted and the tests chosen, the fact that the experiment was primarily in connection with ventilation must be borne in mind. Had the object been merely that of the present research, many differences both in procedure and the tests employed would have been adopted, which would have economised time as well as have simplified the factors involved in the experiment.

Owing to the size of the observation room and the difficulty of controlling its conditions, it was not feasible to test more than four subjects at any one time. The final arrangement was to have six squads of four subjects; each squad to occupy the room for four hours a day on five days of each week. The experiment thus extended over a period of six weeks. The effect of this lengthening of the period will be discussed later; as it is, each squad formed a distinct unit and when its own particular week had elapsed, the results which it gave were complete.

The alteration of the physical conditions of the room, necessary for the ventilation investigation did involve one important psychological factor which is now mentioned. The room in which the experiments were performed was controlled with regard to temperature and humidity. On three days of the week, the temperature was 86° F. accompanied by a humidity of 80%; on the other two days normal conditions of heat and humidity were maintained. The distribution of these days during each particular week was so arranged that the favorable and unfavorable days came in all possible orders during the week period. When the experiments started the effect on mental efficiency of such high temperature and such abnormal humidity was unknown. The results, however, proved that within the limits of experimental error, efficiency when tested by product produced was independent of such external conditions: in other words the subjects achieved quite as much under the hot and humid condition as under normal circumstances. Though the subjects suffered considerable inconvenience and discomfort from the physical condition on three days of the week, yet their scores on these days were as high as when tested under normal conditions—the difference between the two conditions being that of comfort and not that of efficiency. A full statement of these results with the evidence in support is about to be published by the New York State Ventilation Commission. This publication will show that the lack of uniformity in atmospheric conditions need not be considered as a disturbing factor in the present measurements of ability and improvement and their correlations. Even if these results had shown that there was a slight lessening of efficiency under the hot conditions, it would still have been negligible when compared with the unaccountable variations in the individual scores under precisely similar external conditions.

Information Concerning Subjects

The subjects were twenty-two men students of the College of the City of New York. This fact in itself introduces a considerable degree of uniformity in age, education and social status. A record of their age and class is given in the table.

TABLE I
AGE AND CLASS OF SUBJECTS

Individual	Age	College Class
1	16	Freshman
2	20	Senior
3	21	Junior
4	17	Sophomore
5	18	Freshman
6	18	"
7	21	"
8	22	Senior
9	19	Junior
10	19	Freshman
11	18	"
12	18	"
13	18	Sophomore
14	19	Junior
15	18	Freshman
16	20	Sophomore
17	17	Freshman
18	21	Junior
19	20	Sophomore
20	17	Freshman
21	19	Senior
22	18	Sophomore

In this way an artificially selected group of subjects was obtained probably as closely grouped in matters of previous history as could be reasonably expected under any conditions.

It has been observed by every experimenter that the zeal

which the subjects exhibit and the interest which they put into their work is of paramount importance; perhaps along this line of measurement of zeal and satisfyingness of mental work the most interesting results of psychology are to be attained. Unless it is possible to keep this condition of effort or zeal at a constant pitch, the comparison of results is subject to error. It is found that the most advantageous method of standardizing zeal or interest is to keep it at its maximum. In this respect the findings of this research should be of special interest and value; for in every case the subjects were paid for their work. They themselves volunteered for the experiment and seemed to take a keen interest in the scientific side. Added to this stimulus was the knowledge that the employment was on a commercial basis which brought with it an added obligation. Another factor which tended to increase the zeal of the work was the communication to the subjects of the scores of the previous day; this communication added greatly to the interest, often giving rise to an element of friendly rivalry which had a most beneficial effect in reducing the monotony and keeping the zeal at maximum.

No selection of the subjects was made on the basis of general ability. In the preliminary test, however, to qualify for the work it was necessary for each subject to be able to name colors and to perform mental multiplication of three place by three place numbers. This latter test, while it would eliminate a considerable portion of a normal group, did not eliminate a single individual out of a group of thirty chosen from the College of the City of New York. This in itself shows that among these students there has already been operating some considerable selective force. In two cases subjects had to be replaced who were unable to name primary colors; that is, a color test among such a group is more selective than the somewhat difficult operation of mental multiplication of three place numbers.

Before describing the tests employed one advantage of this method which only made it necessary to deal with small groups is worthy of mention. This advantage is the lack of misunderstanding which arises when the tests are administered to but few individuals. After the experiments had once started in no case did results have to be repeated or abandoned because of blunders on the part of the subject.

Description of Tests and Methods of Scoring

The tests used in this experiment ranged from easy association tests to a test of mental efficiency such as is involved in difficult mental multiplication. A description of the nature of these tests will indicate to what extent an identity of elements enters into their composition; between color naming and the opposites test, especially as the latter becomes automatic, there may be marked similarity, but between the mental processes involved in color naming and mental multiplication there can be but little in common. The following is a short description of these tests.

Color Naming Test

The subject was provided with a Woodworth-Wells ('11) blank on which were printed in random order one hundred small squares of varying primary colors; nothing of the nature of discrimination of shades was necessary. The subject was made to name each of the one hundred color squares in as rapid succession as possible. The time taken to name the complete series was measured by the experimenter. In the case of any misnaming of the color the subject was stopped and made to return to the point at which the mistake arose, in this way adding to the time taken for the test. The scores were reduced to product produced, that is, colors named correctly in 100 seconds. In this form the results are stated in the tables.

Cancellation 2 Test

The subject was provided with a Woodworth-Wells ('11) cancellation sheet, in which there are a series of random groupings of five figures. In this sheet a certain specified number, 2 in the first instance, had to be cancelled. The object of the experiment was to omit as few cases of the specified number as possible and to complete a maximum amount of cancellation in the period allowed—60 seconds. The numerical results as given in the tables are calculated on the following arbitrary basis:

2 (number cancelled correctly) — 2 (number omitted)
— 3 (number wrongly marked)

From this method of scoring it will be noticed that additional speed can outweigh complete accuracy. This was pointed out to the subjects at the commencement of the work; the scores from day to day revealing to what extent speed was being gained at the expense of accuracy. The errors are calculated on the above basis:

2 (number omitted) + 3 (number wrongly marked)

and are scored in Table IX.

Cancellation 3 Test

The above test was repeated, cancelling 3's instead of 2's; in all other particulars the two tests were similar. This inclusion of two almost identical functions is of great service as an indication of the reliability of all the coefficents of correlation determined.

Hard Opposites Test

The subject was provided with a list of fifty words as used by Hollingworth ('12), of which the opposites in each case had to be named; a certain range of choice of opposites was allowed. The object of the experiment was to complete this list in a minimum time. In the case of the misnaming of an opposite the subject was stopped and made to return to the point at which the mistake arose. At any time when more than 15 seconds was taken to name any particular opposite, the subject was told the correct word. The time taken to complete the list with the necessary corrections and promptings was measured. After the first test or so, it rarely happened that any prompting was necessary, though throughout, owing to the high speed, occasional mistakes arose. A different arrangement of these words was used in each of these tests. The score as given in the table is reduced to the number of opposites correctly named in a period of 100 seconds.

Addition Test

The subject was provided with two sheets of the set of blanks containing columns of ten one-place numbers as devised by Thorndike ('10).

These same blanks have also been used by Kirby ('13) and others. Different sheets were used from day to day so as to prevent possible memorizing on the part of the subjects.

The object of the test was to complete the maximum number of additions in the time allotted—10 minutes. The answers were written at the base of the columns. If an answer was wrong no credit was given for that column. As in the cancellation tests, it was again pointed out that speed could more than outweigh complete accuracy. The results stated in the tables are the number of columns added correctly in 10 minutes. The number of examples in which errors were made are recorded in Table IX.

Mental Multiplication Test

The subject was provided with a sheet containing a random selection of pairs of three-place numbers arranged by putting any three-place number containing no digit lower than three and repeating no digit, with another such number. These pairs had to be multiplied mentally; nothing being written down until the final product was obtained. The subjects were permitted to look at the problem continuously. The period allowed for the tests was 20 minutes. The method of scoring was as follows: each example done correctly was credited 10, minus 1, 2, 3, 5, for one, two, three, and four figures wrong respectively. Zero credit was given to an example with less than two figures correct. The score recorded in the table is the product in 20 minutes after deduction for errors on the above scale.

Distribution of Time

The tests of which the results are given in the paper were performed each week on a squad of four subjects, on the days from Monday to Friday inclusive. The Saturday previous was devoted to a preliminary trial, in which each squad was put through the series of tests. The rules were explained, while added uniformity was obtained by putting in writing before each subject the object of the test, and the method of scoring. Any questions which arose on the trial day were answered, so that on the days of the test no misunderstanding could arise. By devoting a little time on this preliminary day a great deal of irregularity was avoided in the initial measurements, which is one of the weaknesses of many of the experiments which are performed with big groups with no preliminary training.

Each afternoon of the week was divided into two sections,

the periods falling between 2.30 and 3.45 and 4.15 and 5.30 p.m. respectively. In this manner there were ten periods devoted to the experiment during the five days. During each of these ten periods the whole series of mental tests was employed. The distribution of time meant that the tests were separated by 1¾ and 23 hours. In the tables of scores periods 1 and 2 signify the work of Monday, periods 3 and 4 that of Tuesday, and so on until periods 9 and 10 of Friday. A list of the days on which each subject worked is given Table II.

TABLE II
Program of Work

Individuals 1–22. *Period* Nov. 17, 1912–Feb. 20, 1913

Time periods each day $\begin{cases} 2.30\text{–}3.45 \text{ p.m.} \\ 4.15\text{–}5.30 \text{ p.m.} \end{cases}$

Individuals	Work period
1– 4	Nov. 17–21
5– 8	Dec. 15–19
9–11	Jan. 26–30
12–15	Feb. 2– 6
16–18	Feb. 9–13
19–22	Feb. 16–20

The order of the tests and the time devoted to each during a single period is shown below.

Test	Time spent during each period
Color naming............	Approx. 1½ minutes
Cancellation 2...........	1 "
Cancellation 3...........	1 "
Opposites...............	1½ "
Addition................	10 "
Mental multiplication....	20 "

When the ten periods are considered it will be seen that roughly 15 minutes was devoted to color naming and opposites; 10 minutes each to the cancellation tests; while to addition and mental multiplication the times were 100 minutes and 200 minutes respectively.

Numerical Data

In tables III to VIII the score during each of the ten tests is recorded, the number of the test being indicated in the top horizontal column; the number of the subject in the left-hand vertical column.

TABLE III Scores in Color-naming Test

The scores below are the number of colors named correctly in 100 seconds.

No. of Subject	Tests									
	1	2	3	4	5	6	7	8	9	10
1	200	200	238	227	217	238	213	222	256	270
2	200	217	213	208	208	227	222	244	250	233
3	175	172	204	179	192	208	204	208	208	208
4	179	196	213	196	185	185	182	192	204	196
5	227	232	244	227	244	250	250	256	244	263
6	159	167	192	175	185	185	182	175	185	172
7	200	200	222	222	227	227	238	227	222	217
8	172	179	189	200	200	208	217	217	232	213
9	132	149	159	159	175	169	179	179	182	196
10	222	227	238	238	250	227	244	227	238	204
11	175	185	189	196	208	196	217	192	213	204
12	175	185	179	175	175	172	189	185	200	185
13	244	238	232	227	256	244	208	244	238	270
14	164	172	182	196	170	185	189	208	179	204
15	200	213	192	208	232	208	213	227	244	244
16	222	244	263	263	270	278	303	256	263	250
17	189	208	222	200	250	217	200	200	238	208
18	152	172	170	170	170	179	175	182	196	192
19	222	244	250	227	256	250	278	250	232	256
20	185	204	200	182	208	213	192	200	217	208
21	222	222	238	244	238	256	244	238	238	256
22	213	213	185	204	238	204	213	208	217	217

TABLE IV Scores in Cancellation 2 Test

The scores as shown below are the total products produced in 60 seconds, scored and corrected according to the formula given under the description of the test.

No. of Subject	Tests									
	1	2	3	4	5	6	7	8	9	10
1	88	86	112	108	98	94	112	112	118	116
2	82	94	94	81	94	92	95	104	104	99
3	92	98	110	105	116	116	115	126	111	126
4	100	98	108	113	118	118	130	134	138	144
5	94	94	108	108	108	107	110	113	116	118
6	76	82	100	90	114	104	112	101	116	116
7	102	88	103	112	122	104	122	120	114	118
8	98	104	97	94	122	114	116	114	120	114
9	76	72	78	78	82	90	83	90	84	94
10	67	57	78	78	74	78	82	82	75	84
11	90	100	98	96	96	98	95	90	102	90
12	84	78	82	90	88	90	92	90	98	90
13	62	80	74	100	100	98	110	114	102	106
14	94	96	106	94	116	116	108	116	102	114
15	78	78	80	84	86	92	110	96	100	110
16	84	82	100	86	98	98	102	90	106	116
17	98	96	102	90	108	116	114	112	112	118
18	75	74	70	74	82	72	74	82	84	80
19	82	90	96	122	104	106	114	114	120	118
20	92	104	116	108	118	116	128	128	132	138
21	116	104	116	116	122	122	122	130	120	130
22	110	90	118	116	118	114	118	118	122	118

TABLE V Scores in Cancellation 3 Test

The scores as shown below are the total products produced in 60 seconds scored and corrected according to the formula given under the description of the test.

No. of Subject	1	2	3	4	5	6	7	8	9	10
1	96	112	116	110	102	113	116	104	118	118
2	98	85	102	92	103	104	103	110	110	108
3	88	94	108	94	104	110	104	116	118	109
4	102	108	118	109	122	126	132	130	136	134
5	98	97	110	106	112	114	116	107	122	116
6	82	92	98	94	110	110	114	112	114	110
7	96	103	111	102	112	108	106	112	112	107
8	102	101	102	114	110	116	109	116	110	112
9	72	82	82	92	92	88	88	84	84	84
10	76	72	76	72	82	75	80	82	82	82
11	76	79	96	95	97	92	98	91	98	95
12	90	92	92	98	96	106	98	108	98	110
13	78	78	82	96	98	102	102	104	104	110
14	100	102	100	102	110	106	110	102	108	110
15	80	72	88	90	94	98	98	100	96	102
16	88	96	96	108	100	98	104	110	114	118
17	102	88	102	106	112	110	116	112	118	118
18	68	78	86	76	76	76	78	76	76	78
19	96	92	114	114	114	114	114	126	128	124
20	106	108	118	120	110	116	128	123	136	142
21	112	110	114	116	122	124	126	130	134	130
22	104	98	114	100	114	110	107	108	124	116

TABLE VI Scores in Opposites Test

The score is the number of opposites named correctly in 100 seconds.

No. of Subject	1	2	3	4	5	6	7	8	9	10
1	47	75	77	91	89	104	94	114	104	111
2	35	59	85	93	106	93	100	114	119	135
3	31	30	59	70	98	100	98	114	116	128
4	45	79	96	98	109	104	102	106	119	128
5	53	104	116	109	119	125	147	156	139	139
6	43	66	98	93	98	96	109	119	98	102
7	48	40	64	63	77	91	93	91	106	104
8	50	53	88	75	94	104	104	114	111	102
9	36	56	78	75	83	89	98	104	100	114
10	41	63	67	74	71	82	86	77	85	86
11	56	59	72	83	85	91	93	82	91	91
12	82	89	94	119	125	79	122	132	135	143
13	64	83	102	106	135	119	139	109	119	135
14	26	42	45	56	89	65	106	96	104	102
15	30	63	83	82	96	91	94	89	104	106
16	65	85	98	109	109	132	139	122	139	147
17	46	77	104	91	98	119	114	122	109	125
18	48	63	75	76	76	78	86	83	109	100
19	41	82	100	111	125	125	135	132	147	147
20	63	77	85	91	94	94	102	111	114	116
21	68	79	67	89	100	106	122	116	135	135
22	77	93	100	106	125	135	114	128	128	132

TABLE VII Scores in Addition Test

The score is the number of columns added correctly in 10 minutes.

No. of Subject					Tests					
	1	2	3	4	5	6	7	8	9	10
1	80	81	96	98	98	85	95	88	104	96
2	55	55	58	59	66	65	60	65	72	79
3	82	82	96	93	100	106	103	104	107	110
4	50	52	51	54	61	53	56	58	68	60
5	91	103	108	109	118	124	131	135	134	137
6	68	78	78	86	88	98	94	92	97	99
7	72	72	74	72	64	69	75	81	75	85
8	92	96	102	101	106	105	108	111	119	114
9	38	36	41	47	47	52	55	57	57	62
10	39	40	48	46	50	52	57	56	57	56
11	47	46	45	48	50	51	48	55	53	55
12	52	66	72	75	78	78	91	86	91	91
13	68	69	75	73	82	83	86	89	105	100
14	68	58	53	64	60	62	68	65	60	74
15	54	58	69	62	60	69	68	73	80	72
16	55	54	58	65	63	57	57	69	78	74
17	45	44	48	47	55	60	62	63	64	66
18	39	44	41	53	45	47	50	52	53	51
19	90	93	103	107	104	104	116	117	118	119
20	64	69	85	78	84	84	94	91	86	98
21	62	61	69	69	77	75	79	80	81	81
22	58	65	71	65	70	73	72	79	81	83

TABLE VIII Scores in Mental Multiplication Test

The scores as shown below are the total products produced in 20 minutes, scored and corrected according to the formula given under the description of the test.

No. of Subject					Tests					
	1	2	3	4	5	6	7	8	9	10
1	35	40	48	60	44	85	65	93	60	108
2	33	49	48	58	55	67	69	70	79	98
3	50	49	65	75	79	85	92	97	90	98
4	35	34	52	56	79	75	88	63	67	73
5	42	36	45	45	61	54	60	63	65	70
6	35	47	41	60	71	68	79	58	77	88
7	13	17	15	21	44	26	40	20	30	25
8	20	28	38	45	52	46	58	60	66	65
9	40	37	39	49	50	48	50	41	56	70
10	40	56	38	55	74	60	80	75	78	84
11	28	31	19	38	24	42	14	45	55	67
12	9	36	33	34	50	52	61	66	59	66
13	49	52	72	71	85	74	70	80	78	102
14	70	70	85	90	74	92	100	106	116	102
15	50	74	84	79	92	105	86	107	98	118
16	53	65	62	78	74	78	69	87	78	87
17	34	37	29	46	45	44	61	55	50	52
18	33	33	34	31	46	36	42	45	36	43
19	40	38	44	43	54	39	47	54	58	47
20	27	50	47	57	69	77	66	78	78	88
21	44	44	64	71	75	95	96	105	96	105
22	26	59	69	98	83	81	88	102	86	90

TABLE IX
SCORE OF ERRORS IN CANCELLATION AND ADDITION TESTS

The errors are the total produced during the complete series of tests, scored on the basis given in the description of the respective tests.

No. of Subject	Can. 2	Can. 3	Addition	No. of Subject	Can. 2	Can. 3	Addition
1	10	12	13	12	4	2	31
2	18	13	24	13	6	6	41
3	21	15	27	14	12	10	64
4	27	7	79	15	6	2	45
5	14	8	49	16	2	0	25
6	7	2	64	17	10	0	75
7	25	42	49	18	15	6	56
8	17	17	67	19	0	0	20
9	9	4	24	20	10	13	86
10	12	6	53	21	6	2	53
11	15	29	66	22	0	9	49

Effects of Practise

The measurement of the scores of the subjects in each test over ten periods shows some interesting results concerning the general form of the practise curves in each of the different functions. If, taking any single test, such as color naming or addition, the total score during each of the ten tests is obtained and then divided by 22, and these scores plotted as ordinates against time, or rather the number of the test, as abscissa, a type of curve is obtained which is a composite or average of all the various curves. The curve of each subject is far too unreliable to give anything but a rough idea of the general shape of the curve, but by compounding a fairly accurate knowledge can be gained. See curves on page 14. The marked differences between the form of the curves become at once apparent. In the color test even though only 15 minutes has been spent in practise, there is a rapid rise which is followed by a flattening or rapid decrease in the rate of improvement after the sixth period. The curve shows that half the final gain is scored by the end of two periods after the initial score.

In the case of the cancellation practise curve there is a much greater approximation to a rectilinear relation, but here again there is evident towards the end of the practise a slight flattening of the curve. Half the final gain is reached at the end of 3.5 periods after the initial score.

In general shape the opposites curve resembles the color curve, indicating the similarity in the relative rate of improvement in the two functions. But in the case of the opposites

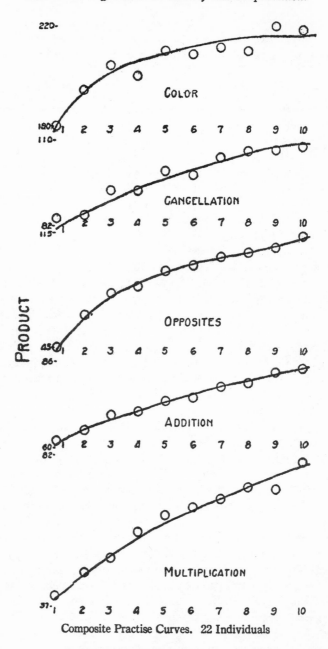

Composite Practise Curves.   22 Individuals

there is less decrease in rate of improvement than in the color test; half the final gain is reached at the end of 2.5 periods after the initial score.

The addition and mental multiplication practise curves, apart from small irregularities, are approximately rectilinear, indicating a steady rise of efficiency with little decrease in improvability even at the end of the practise periods of 100 and 200 minutes respectively. Half the final gains are reached in 4 and 3.5 periods after the initial score in the case of these two curves.

It is obvious that we can arrange these practise curves in order with relation to the extent to which they give a rectilinear relation between product produced and time spent in practise. The color and opposites curves may be classified together. In each of these cases, as was to be expected, there is a rapid rise accompanied by a decided falling off in the rate of improvement towards the end of the times of practise. This is what is known to happen in any function which rapidly becomes automatic; in both tests the functions are too narrow to allow a long continued improvement to be made.

The cancellation curve is of a type intermediate between the color and opposites curves, and that found in the case of addition. This function admits of less rapid improvement and, therefore, in the same time as is devoted to the color test, does not show the same decrease in rate of improvement. The fact is well brought out in the diagrams.

When we compare this curve with that obtained by Wells ('12) with his ten subjects, five men and five women, in a marking number test, it is at once apparent that there is almost complete similarity between the results. In his experiments during a period of 20 minutes, which, counting the time devoted to both tests, is the time spent on cancellation in these experiments, there is a slight initial rise in the rate of improvement, followed towards the end of the period by the same decrease in improvability.

The addition curve is again intermediate in form between that found in the cancellation test and that obtained in mental multiplication. There would be in the case of addition, owing to its more complex nature, a much greater range of improvement than in such a simple test as cancellation. Previous training would also have its effect on the scores. In a much trained function, such as addition, the initial rate of improvement would be less relatively to the later rate than in a strange test such as cancellation.

The addition curve shows a slight dissimilarity from that obtained by Wells ('12) using the same ten subjects. Over a period of 100 minutes, the time used in this experiment, he finds a more rapid rise with a tendency to a greater decrease in rate of improvability towards the end of the period. It is comparatively easy to account for the more rapid initial rise, for in his experiments the subjects were nurses of ages between 21 and 35. These subjects would certainly not have had or be in such practise as the subjects in this experiment, who at the time were reading for a degree, and who must therefore have already attained considerable efficiency in such a simple test as addition. Possibly also, in the case of Wells's subjects the difficulty of adaptation to the work was greater than in the case of college students.

The more pronounced flattening of his curves towards the end of the period is possibly to be explained by lack of power of concentration. He himself noted that the monotony of the experiments materially affected his subjects. In no case in these experiments was this at all evident. The effect of monotony if not overcome by extra effort on the part of the subject would produce the slightly greater decrease in rate of improvement found in his study.

In the practise curve of the mental multiplication test there is a noticeable difference in form. This is due to the fact that over a period of 200 minutes there is little possibility of the subjects reaching the limit of their improvement. The complexity of the function combined with little previous practise would allow great range, so that in this case even at the end of the period the curve should still be rising rapidly. This is found to be the case, after a slight initial acceleration in improvement, the curve becoming rectilinear and continuing so till the end of the period. This agrees with what Thorndike ('08) found in measuring the same function.

It may be interesting to state here the actual percentage improvement recorded by all the individuals when averages are taken in the manner previously described: this is found by adding up the total products during the first and last periods. These scores are divided by 22. The first column of the following table states the nature of the test, the second the average initial score, the third the gross average improvement, the fourth gives the percentage improvement, while the fifth records the time spent in practise reckoning from the middle of the first to the middle of the last test.

TABLE X

TABLE OF AVERAGE INITIAL SCORES AND GROSS AND
PERCENTAGE IMPROVEMENTS

Average for individuals 1–22 obtained by summation from previous tables.

Test	Initial score	Gross improvement	Percentage improvement	Minutes spent in practise
Color................	189	28	15	14
Cancellation 2........	84	23	27	19
Opposites............	45	70	156	14
Addition.............	62	22	36	90
Mental multiplication.	37	43	116	180

The large percentage improvement in the opposites test is largely due to the method of scoring. In all cases of measurements of improvement of these simple functions, the difficulty of scoring is great for, owing to the law of decreasing returns, a unit gained at the end of the practise period may be worth many units gained at the commencement. This would be particularly true of the opposites test.

The large gain in mental multiplication reveals how little a prolonged general training does for a particular mental operation. That an average subject in 180 minutes should improve 116 per cent after approximately 15 years of experience with numbers suggests the specialisation which takes place in mental functions.

Practise Curves of Individuals in the Tests

Whenever the efficiency of an individual in any test is measured at stated intervals so as to obtain a practise curve, the first thing that strikes the attention is the great irregularity exhibited by such a curve. In order to investigate this irregularity, four individual records have been chosen at random, and the form of the practise curves for each of these tests plotted. Owing to the variations in the extent of improvement in each function shown by each individual, the scale of ordinates of each of the following graphs has been so chosen that the curves showing the improvement rise to approximately the same height. This has necessitated the use of arbitrary scales. In the general case it may be said that the maximum ordinate represents the total improvement. The scores produced during each of the ten trials are plotted by taking equidistant points along the abscissa to represent the ten periods at which measurements were made. It should be noted that the curves are not drawn from the zero line. The figures on the left of each curve indicate the ordinate values, the figures on the right are the improvement measured by subtracting the initial from the final score.

Instead of a steady rise and a smooth curve such as results with composite practise curves, the various points forming the curve are distributed in a very irregular manner, though in all cases they give a general indication of the improvability of the function. These variabilities from test to test are well brought out in the curves shown in the diagrams. In drawing certain of the curves where a rapid initial rise took place, as in the opposites test, the first point in the curve is not included. On the right hand side there is recorded the gross gain measured by subtracting the score of the first from the score of the last period. These improvements in the same time show marked individual differences. For these four individuals chosen at random the gains in the color test are 70, 33, 13, and 23, while for the same individuals the gains in addition are 16, 28, 31, and 34 respectively. These values in themselves give some idea of the range of differences found in rate of improvement in a homogeneous group.

Since each of the tests was performed during the same period, that is, within the same hour, it is a matter of interest to determine whether the fluctuations shown by the curves are actually due to a prolonged alteration in general efficiency, or whether the conditions out of which they arise are merely of a momentary character. If the first theory is true,—that it is a prolonged decrease in general efficiency at any one time which accounts for the decrease in product produced during the test, then this decrease in mental efficiency should operate in all the tests. When the various curves are compared, at a point where there is a decrease in product in one function, there should also

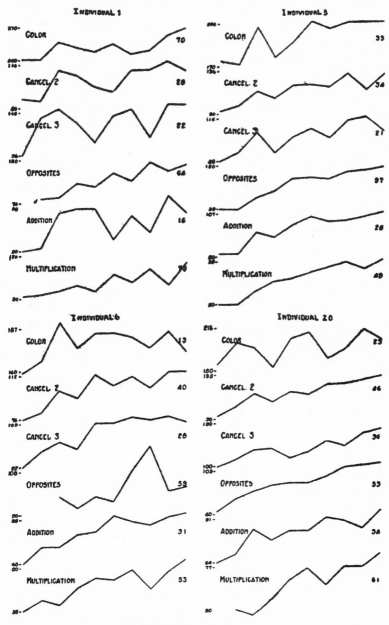

Individual Practise Curves
Practise Curves for 4 Typical Individuals.
Arbitrary Scale for Ordinates. See text.

be a decrease in product in all the other functions. On the other hand if the conditions determining the efficiency of a subject are of merely temporary duration, no such relation would be found between the variations in scoring powers in different tests.

A comparison of the curves fails to reveal any such regularity; a minimum point obtained in any single test does not seem to be accompanied by minimum points in the other tests except to the extent which a random distribution will explain. If the curves of further individuals are plotted, they bear out the same point. It should be noted, however, that these tests were not performed simultaneously: only under these circumstances would it be justifiable to assume that decrease in efficiency in one test is not necessarily connected with decrease in efficiency in other tests. All that these results actually demonstrate is that the conditions which are responsible for low scores in one test either do not operate when other tests are concerned or else the conditions do not last for a sufficient time to affect the tests spread over the time in question. With regard to the first of these assumptions, the relation between the curves for the cancellation 2 and the cancellation 3 test is especially instructive, for not only were these tests performed within one-half minute of each other, but they are also sufficiently similar to assume that they correspond to almost identical mental processes. Even under these conditions, no relation is apparent between the two curves—a great rise in the cancellation 2 curve is not invariably accompanied by a rise in the cancellation 3 curve. In the diagrams shown there are several cases where the reverse is the truth.

These considerations can lead to but one conclusion, namely, that the conditions which affect efficiency, unless they are very extreme, such as severe headache, are so temporary or so specialized that they do not influence other tests of a similar and dissimilar nature. Although in terms of the neurones there must be explanations for these alterations in zeal or efficiency, the variations obtained would, as far as the actual score is concerned, appear to be of a random nature.

The subjects discussed by Wells ('12) in his paper on the relation of practise to individual differences could be treated here from the general form of the curves of each individual, if it were possible to draw these curves with sufficient precision when such few points are determined, and such large variations occur. Wells found with nearly all his subjects that high initial efficiency in no way precluded the expectation of considerable practise improvement. He was, however, unable to draw any general conclusions from his limited measurements. The whole subject is much better adapted to statistical than graphical treatment. The demonstration of such a fact that high initial efficiency was usually the accompaniment of great improvability, by means of curves, would be laborious and inelegant. The more adequate method of treating these facts is by means of a study of correlations. This subject will, therefore, now be discussed.

Method of Calculating the Correlations

The concomitant variation between two mental character-istics, such as the efficiency of a group of individuals in two particular tests, is capable of expression in one single coefficient of correlation. This coefficient of correlation is a figure so calculated from a number of individual measurements as to represent the general trend of the relation between the two variable qualities of a group. The coefficient may have all possible values from $+1$ through 0 to -1, these numerical values indicating perfect correspondence, random relationship, and perfect opposition respectively.

Several methods of calculating the coefficient of correlation present themselves, the method adopted in any particular case depending upon the nature and accuracy of the result required. Throughout this research the foot-rule or R method devised by Spearman will be used. While this method does not give the precise relative weight to each individual measurement, the results which can be rapidly obtained from its use are accurate enough for the purposes of the present investigation.

This particular coefficient has been used sufficiently by other experimenters to warrant its adoption in this case. Any further discussion of its merits and demerits can be found in the original paper by Spearman ('04). Adopting the usual notation, if R denotes the first coefficient, the formula used is:

$$R = 1 - \frac{6\,\Sigma G}{n^2 - 1}$$

where $\Sigma G =$ sum of the plus differences in ranks and $n =$

number of cases in the series.   These values of R obtained directly from the differences in rank can readily be converted into terms of r, the coefficient of correlation, according to tables expressing the relation.

$$r = \sin \left[\frac{\pi}{2}\right] R.$$

These formulae have been used throughout the whole of this study; in every case the values of R have been converted into terms of r, even in the case when R has a negative value.

Reliability of the Coefficients

Whenever a coefficient of correlation is calculated from a finite number of measurements, there is admitted a source of error.   Using the method of ranks it is not legitimate to determine the probable error on the basis of the more complete formula for the r method.   Such a determination will, however, give at any rate the order of the reliability, so that with this limitation and precaution we may assume:

$$\text{P.E.} = \frac{.6745}{\sqrt{n}} (1 - r^2)$$

where r = actual coefficient of correlation.

n = no. of cases included.   In every case in this paper $n = 22$, so that

$$\text{P.E.} = \frac{.6745}{\sqrt{22}} (1 - r^2)$$

The significance of any single coefficient of correlation can be determined in the light of the following table.

TABLE XI

PROBABLE ERROR OF THE COEFFICIENT OF CORRELATION

USING FORMULA: $\text{P.E.} = \dfrac{.67 (1 - r^2)}{\sqrt{n}}$

r	Group $n = 22$ P.E.
.1	.14
.2	.13
.3	.13
.4	.12
.5	.10
.6	.09
.7	.07
.8	.05
.9	.03

Correction for Attenuation

In order to correct for the attenuation of the coefficient of correlation by chance error in the data, it is necessary to have at least two independent scores of the particular traits to be measured. If these can be found, one method of procedure is as follows:

Suppose A and B to be the series to be related.

Let p be a series of exact measures of A.

Let q be a series of exact measures of B.

p_1 and p_2 be two independent series of measures of A

q_1 and q_2 be two independent series of measures of B

then, with the usual notation, a more probable correlation is shown,

$$r\,p\,q = \frac{\sqrt{r\,p_1\,q_2 \times r\,p_2\,q_1}}{\sqrt{r\,p_1\,p_2 \times r\,q_1\,q_2}}$$

To use this formula it is necessary to have two independent series of measures of each function. This independence cannot be assumed in this research where the practise effect enters; theoretically the formula is only applicable in the case where the practise effect is absent, that is, when we are measuring a mental characteristic which apart from normal fluctuations is static. This consideration prevents any attempt at an accurate correction of the raw coefficients. In spite of this, however, in most cases the necessary coefficients for the purposes of this correction will be calculated, not so that they may be used directly for giving an accurate attenuation correction but rather that they may indicate in a general way the order of the allowance which must be made for chance errors in the data.

Correlation Between Initial Abilities in the Various Functions

Most of the experiments which have been made to determine the relation between efficiencies in different mental characteristics have measured the efficiencies at one stated period of time, the efficiency being the product of original nature and all the diverse previous training. In making the tests on the subjects the time periods have been so distributed or of so short length that the practise effect has not seriously affected the results. In the present work it will be seen from the form of the curves shown earlier in the paper, that there is a considerable improvement factor. Since this is the case, any measurements obtained are not strictly initial abilities, for they represent the initial efficiency in the function together with a certain addition due to practise. Thus, for example, if we accept as the measure of initial ability the sum of the products produced during the first three periods, a reference to the practise curves in each case will reveal the extent to which this single measurement is a compound of the initial ability, due to previous training, with a corresponding ability acquired during the period over which the tests extended. Theoretically if a true measure of initial ability is to be obtained, the test period must be exceedingly short; the shorter the period the more practise may be expected to enter. The other method is to separate the trials by such long periods that the practise effect is destroyed by time. If, however, a single measurement of efficiency is taken, say the product produced during the first test alone, the gain in definition of initial efficiency is more than lost by the chance errors which enter into any single measurement of a score. When the total product of the first three tests is assumed to represent the initial efficiency a much more accurate determination is obtained, but it is necessary to remember the meaning which attaches to initial ability when estimated in this way.

If the raw correlations between initial abilities in the different tests are to be corrected for attenuation, it is necessary that two independent measures be made of this so-called initial ability. Such measures for the direct application of the attenuation formula cannot be obtained for the reasons previously given, but at the same time, though the measurements are not independent, the raw correlations obtained from them will enable a rough correction to be made which will give a much truer idea of the correlations existing than do the raw coefficients themselves.

For purposes of general convenience in connection with the rest of the paper, the first measure of initial efficiency from which the coefficients of correlation are determined will be the sum of the scores during tests $(1+2+3)$; the second measure the score produced during tests $(4+5)$. If these summation products are calculated from the tables in the case of each of the tests and then arranged in rank order, the following are the raw Spearman intercorrelation coefficients, arranged in a table of the usual form. The figures (1+2+3) represent the score of the first three tests, while (4+5) represent the same product for the fourth and fifth tests.

TABLE XII
CORRELATION BETWEEN INITIAL SCORES

Individuals 1–22. Measures of initial score. (1) sum (1+2+3) tests (2) sum (4+5) tests

	Color (1+2+3) tests	Color (4+5) tests	Cancellation 2 (1+2+3) tests	Cancellation 2 (4+5) tests	Cancellation 3 (1+2+3) tests	Cancellation 3 (4+5) tests	Opposites (1+2+3) tests	Opposites (4+5) tests	Addition (1+2+3) tests	Addition (4+5) tests	Mental multiplication (1+2+3) tests	Mental multiplication (4+5) tests
Color: (1+2+3)		.92	-.02	.11	.19	.29	.28	.25	.32	.31	.32	.14
(4+5)				.09		.19		.32		.26		.22
Cancellation 2: (1+2+3)				.78	.84	.75	.22	.06	.35	.34	.03	.16
(4+5)						.87		.30		.54		.00
Cancellation 3: (1+2+3)						.89	.19	-.02	.45	.43	-.13	-.05
(4+5)								.35		.48		-.14
Opposites: (1+2+3)								.83	.08	.20	.09	.16
(4+5)										.25		.25
Addition: (1+2+3)										.97	-.02	-.02
(4+5)												.02
Mental multiplication: (1+2+3)												
(4+5)												.92

The value of the correlations in the same test between the scores of the (1+2+3) tests and the (4+5) tests indicates the order of the correction which has to be applied to the raw coefficients to correct for attenuation. There is also another check upon the chance errors which enter into the determination of these coefficients. This is obtained by examining the correlations between the initial efficiencies in the two cancellation tests. As far as it is possible to obtain identical tests, these two tests are similar. For this reason it is legitimate to assume that the correlation factors found to be .87 and .75 would, if chance errors were eliminated, approach unity. When the attenuation correction is applied directly using the formula explained in a previous section, the correlation becomes

$$r = \frac{\sqrt{87 \times 75}}{\sqrt{78 \times 89}} = .97.$$

This value would to a certain extent justify the use of this formula under these special conditions. Without actually employing the full attenuation correction, a close approximation to the correct value of the coefficients of correlation is obtained if each value is interpreted in the light of the fact that an almost perfect correlation as exhibited in the cancellation tests is of the order .8.

When these coefficients are examined and allowance is made for the attenuation by raising each coefficient, it will at once be seen that apart from the correlation between the almost identical cancellation tests, the average coefficient is lower than that obtained in most of the previous experiments. This lowness of the coefficient is evidence of the lack of similarity between the various mental traits examined. We can also view these low values from another point of view. Many of the high correlations obtained in previous studies, especially when the subjects were school children, are to a certain extent the result of a general power to understand instructions and a power of adaptation to the conditions of the experiment. Thus a subject who had this general power would tend to be efficient in all the tests while the child slow to grasp instructions would show but slight ability throughout; both cases in this way would contribute to a high correlation. There is little doubt, especially with measurements on large groups, that this factor is responsible for many of the high uniform results obtained. With the subjects of this study such a general intelligence factor would hardly enter. Ability to understand instructions which were of the simplest kind can be presupposed; even if small misunderstandings did arise, these happened on the preliminary trial day, the scores of which are not included in the research. In addition to this, it is to be remembered that this group was highly selected; had it been less homogeneous naturally much larger correlations would have resulted.

A consideration of the grouping of the coefficients is perhaps the most instructive method of summarizing the main results.

If we take each of the functions and determine by summation and averaging the correlation with all other functions combined, the following results are obtained.

TABLE XIII

AVERAGE CORRELATION OF INITIAL SCORES IN EACH TEST WITH
ALL THE REMAINING TESTS
(Deduced from Table XII)

Tests	Average coefficient of correlation with every other function
Color	.22
	(not including Can. 3)
Cancellation 2	.18
	(not including Can. 2)
Cancellation 3	.19
Opposites	.20
Addition	.27
Mental multiplication	.06

After raising these coefficients to correct for attenuation it is evident that there is a definite positive correlation in the case of the color naming, cancellation, opposites and addition tests, while with mental multiplication the average correlation with the other functions is of much lower order, but still positive. This last result is of special significance. It might appear that if the mental multiplication operation could be performed at all, it would necessarily accompany a high level of intelligence which would carry with it an efficiency in all other functions. Certainly *a priori* considerations would lead to this view; in this case the subject who was exceptional in such a rigorous test would show superiority in all the other tests. That such is not the case is obvious from the last figure recorded, .06. The explanation for such a low correlation is to be found in supposing that the power of performing such a task is highly specialised. The other tests are largely motor or direct association; in mental multiplication, which is a purely intellectual test, the chief factors concerned are memory and concentration. The apparent similarity between the addition and the mental multiplication test is deceptive, the arithmetic of the latter test being of negligible importance when compared with the demand made upon memory.

These results may be compared briefly with those found in previous experiments. Unfortunately, tests similar to those of this study have not been extensively used. Spearman ('04), as a result of his experiments, reached results which justified him in supposing that there exist powers which may be termed: " general sensory discrimination and general intelligence." Later, Spearman and Krueger ('06) published an investigation of the correlations existing among the following abilities: touch discrimination, tone discrimination, adding, learning by heart a series of numbers, Ebbinghaus mutilated texts. The subjects were eleven university students. The raw coefficients obtained were of a slightly higher order than those found in this research, but in several cases, such as the correlations between learning by heart and the Ebbinghaus test, learning by heart and touch discrimination, negative correlations were obtained. Spearman and Krueger again conclude that there is a distinct positive correlation between abilities of the range they measured.

That no such high correlation can exist between sensory discrimination and general intelligence was shown by Thorndike ('09). These results are generally supported by those of Burt ('09). It is only when we come to the results obtained by Brown ('09) and Hollingworth ('13) that it is possible to make any comparison of the numerical results, and even here such comparison is limited. The accuracy of Brown's results is greater than my own, owing to the greater number of individuals examined as well as the absence of the practise effect. Brown found for the correlation between marking letters and addition, using the Pearson coefficient a series of values for the three groups: .59, .13, .35, .51, .00, .20; the values for this study of the relation between cancellation and addition tests are .35, .34, .54, .45, .43 and .48. The wide range of values obtained by Brown shows how great is the danger of arguing from any determination of correlation coefficients in a single group. In his three groups there could be but small differences, as is indicated by the following particulars:

Group 1.—66 boys of a London elementary school, all between the ages of 11 and 12.

Group 2.—39 girls of a London elementary school, all between the ages of 11 and 12.

Group 3.—40 boys of a London higher grade school, all between the ages of 11 and 12.

Yet between mechanical memory and addition the correlations exhibited by these three groups are .27, —.13 and .00 respectively. This in itself shows the small reliability which can be placed even upon careful determinations of somewhat large homogeneous groups.

In a paper recently published by Hollingworth ('13), the author has determined the correlations over a long period of practise with thirteen individuals in some of the tests used in this study. If we take the correlations between initial abilities in the tests in common to both experiments, a comparison of results can be made. In the case of the three following pairs of tests his values for the correlation are shown in the first column, while those of this study are shown in the second:

Pairs of tests	Hollingworth	Present results
Color naming and opposites......	.60	.28
Color naming and addition.......	.11	.30
Opposites and addition..........	.20	.17

The similarity between these results is perhaps as great as can be expected from such measurements. In connection with this same research, the details of which are too complex to give, Hollingworth concludes that the average correlations of all the tests become positive and the coefficients become greater the longer the practise is continued. To what extent this rise in the correlation is due to less chance error in the data, the paper does not allow one to judge. This certainly must be a factor in the increase.

Simpson's ('12) monograph on the correlation of mental abilities, in addition to an account of his own experiments, also adds a useful summary of the more important recent studies. In all, he uses 15 tests of a simple nature such as could be applied to a group of low mental order. If we confine our attention to the superior group of high academic standing, in these fifteen tests, the correlation for the superior group rarely rises above .5 and has an average value of between .2 and .3. This is essentially the same result as that found in the present study. Simpson concludes: "We find justification for the common assumption that there is a close interrelation among certain mental abilities, and consequently something that may be called general mental ability or general intelligence; and that on the other hand certain capacities are relatively specialized and do not necessarily imply other abilities except to a limited extent."

The conclusion reached by Brown in his study, just referred to, is typical of all the experiments: "the correlation between different psychical abilities is not very close, and few correlations are greater than .6." This conclusion is supported by the results of this paper; in fact, his correlation of .6 would appear to be high. If we assume a correlation after correction of about .3 as a maximum, and .2 as a minimum between all the mental tests of this study, there is every probability that this gives a true estimate of the actual correlations between the mental abilities tested in the case of these twenty-two individuals.

Correlation Between Initial and Final Scores

Another series of correlations throws an interesting light on the form of the practise curves of individuals in the various tests. Wells ('12) in his paper on the relation of practise to individual differences has in the case of addition and number checking tests plotted the practise curves of his ten subjects. In the addition test over 30 five-minute periods, save in one case the subjects consistently maintained the same order of efficiency given in the initial performance. In other words, the curves spread out fan shape, rarely intersecting one another. The same maintenance of relative order throughout the tests takes place in the number checking experiment. This conclusion with regard to the maintenance of relative order which he deduces graphically can be investigated statistically for the 22 individuals of this study. For this purpose all that is necessary is to adopt some suitable measure of initial and final abilities. If the relative order is maintained throughout the test the correlation between initial and final scores should be of a high order; if, on the other hand, there are great changes in the relative positions of the individuals, the correlation should be distinctly low.

In the following table, the initial score is defined as the product produced during the first three tests, while the measure of the final score is the sum of the scores of the last two trials. By taking these two averages rather than the first and last score, a considerable amount of reliability is gained in the measures. Especially at the commencement of each test, there are very liable to be great irregularities, such as if used in measuring correlation would necessitate a high attenuation factor for correction. Column 1 shows the function in question, column 2 the correlation between the early and late scores as defined.

TABLE XIV

CORRELATION BETWEEN EARLY AND LATE SCORES

early score = scores (1+2+3) tests
late score = scores (9+10) tests

Test	Correlation coefficient
Color........................	.87
Cancellation 2.................	.75
Cancellation 3.................	.85
Opposites.....................	.59
Addition......................	.96
Multiplication................	.87

In the 22 individuals tested, there is then, even in the raw coefficients, an exceptionally high correlation between early and late scores. In the addition test the correlation rises to the abnormally high value of .96, while with the exception of the opposites test, which at all times is irregular, the least value is in cancellation 2 which gives .75. The uncertainty of all such measurements is shown by the values of the coefficients in the two cancellation tests, which apart from chance errors should have an equal value. The maintenance of relative order throughout the tests which was found by Wells is therefore fully supported by the results of these experiments. Similar results of a lower order in tests of weight discrimination, marking letters, sorting and multiplication were found by Whitley ('11).

The distinction between initial and final score correlations and of initial score and absolute gain correlations should not be confused. Because an individual has the greatest initial as well as the largest final score does not necessarily imply that he has gained more than any other individual; quite the reverse may be the truth. This relationship between initial ability and improvement will be discussed later.

Correlation of Improvability in One Function with
Improvability in Other Functions

Of all the problems of individual differences which yet await solution, none is of greater interest than that concerned with the general improvability of individuals in various functions.

If it is true that an individual who over a certain specified time gains a certain amount in one test is likely to gain a certain corresponding amount in other tests and if with many subjects this correlation is high, we shall be able to arrange individuals in order of merit with regard to general improvability, in this way obtaining a criterion for the selection of those persons who are likely to benefit most by education.

In order to gain an idea of the correction for attenuation two measurements of improvement are calculated

   (1) scores (6+7+8) tests — scores (1+2+3) tests
   (2) scores (9+10) tests   — scores (4+5) tests

These two scores of the improvement can be regarded as the early and late improvement respectively. The form of the practise curves shown in an earlier part of the paper explains

TABLE XV

Correlation Between Improvabilities

Individuals 1–22.   *Measure of improvement.*

              (1) score (6+7+8) — score (1+2+3)
              (2) score (9+10)   — score (4+5)

	Color (9+10) — (4+5)	Cancellation 2 (6+7+8) — (1+2+3)	Cancellation 2 (9+10) — (4+5)	Cancellation 3 (6+7+8) — (1+2+3)	Cancellation 3 (9+10) — (4+5)	Opposites (6+7+8) — (1+2+3)	Opposites (9+10) — (4+5)	Addition (6+7+8) — (1+2+3)	Addition (9+10) — (4+5)	Mental multiplication (6+7+8) — (1+2+3)	Mental multiplication (9+10) — (4+5)
Color:											
(6+7+8) — (1+2+3)	.19	−.22	−.03	−.26	−.19	.56	.63	−.17	−.13	−.41	.02
(9+10) — (4+5)		−.32	.37	.05	−.06	.05	.14	−.14	.02	.02	.37
Cancellation 2:											
(6+7+8) — (1+2+3)			.35	**.66**	**.20**	.14	−.05	.28	.20	.17	−.08
(9+10) — (4+5)				**.50**	**.55**	.02	.08	.13	.14	.25	.22
Cancellation 3:											
(6+7+8) — (1+2+3)					.31	.08	−.11	.40	.44	.22	.13
(9+10) — (4+5)						.17	.17	.14	.03	.60	−.02
Opposites:											
(6+7+8) — (1+2+3)							.65	.26	.31	−.25	−.11
(9+10) — (4+5)								−.06	−.17	−.16	−.16
Addition:											
(6+7+8) — (1+2+3)									.40	.08	−.02
(9+10) — (4+5)										−.09	−.17
Mental multiplication:											
(6+7+8) — (1+2+3)											.48
(9+10) — (4+5)											

the significance which should be attached to each of these measures of improvability. In no case is the score of the gain estimated from a single period. Initially the single estimate score (10–1) test was used. Although in this way a larger gain is introduced, the uncertainty due to chance errors in the initial and final scores is so great as to make the results of little value. It is of much greater advantage to sacrifice a small amount of numerical improvement, in order to get a more reliable measure of what this gain actually is. With the color and opposites tests in which the practise curves exhibit a rapid rise in efficiency with a corresponding decrease in improvability during the later periods, the arbitrary nature of the gains as measured by any one score is apparent. Where the practise curve does not approach a straight line, the actual values of the coefficient of correlation must of necessity be affected by the range over which the practise extends. The correlation between each pair of functions is calculated in the four possible ways, if the average of these coefficients is taken a fair approximation to the correct result for the raw coefficient can be assumed.

For purposes of easy reference, the average intercorrelation between each pair of tests is deduced from Table XV.

TABLE XVI

AVERAGE CORRELATION BETWEEN IMPROVABILITIES
(Deduced from Table XV)

	Color	Can. 2	Can. 3	Opp.	Add.	Mul.
Color..............	.....	—.05	—.12	.35	—.11	.00
Cancellation 2......			.48	.05	.19	.14
Cancellation 3......				.08	.25	.23
Opposites..........					.09	—.17
Addition...........						—.05
Multiplication......						

The interpretation of these tables is somewhat difficult. Not to apply any correction for attenuation in the cases where it is possible is certainly to minimize the value of the results. The correction for attenuation, however, becomes unsuitable when the correlations are very low or of negative value. Perhaps the best method is to make no use of the attenuation correction but to consider the values of the correlations between the gains in the cancellation 2 and the cancellation 3 tests.

The almost complete identity of elements which exists between these two operations justifies the assumption that apart from chance errors in the data, the coefficient should be almost unity. The actual value of this raw coefficient, if we take the average of the four determinations, is .48. This indicates that apart from errors which must enter, especially in the measurement of improvement, a correlation of approximately .5 represents a true correlation of approximately unity. If each one of these coefficients when of sufficiently high value above zero is interpreted with this in mind, something approaching a true estimate of correct values may be obtained. When the coefficients approach zero or are of negative value no correction should be made.

Apart from the correlation between the two cancellation tests the only other pairs which give anything approaching a high correlation are (1) the color and opposites tests, (2) the addition and cancellation tests. Possibly in the color and opposites tests there may be present identical elements, but this explanation can hardly explain the relation between addition and cancellation.

If the same procedure is adopted in dealing with the correlations between improvements as was adopted in the case of the correlations between initial efficiencies and we take an average of all the coefficients of correlation which are obtained when comparing any particular test with all the other tests, the following are the results obtained.

TABLE XVII
AVERAGE CORRELATION OF IMPROVABILITIES IN EACH TEST WITH
ALL THE REMAINING TESTS
(Deduced from Table XV)

Test	Average correlation with all other tests
Color......................	.01 (not including Can. 3)
Cancellation 2...............	.08 (not including Can. 2)
Cancellation 3...............	.11
Opposites...................	.08
Addition....................	.09
Mental multiplication.........	.03

This table at once reveals the absence of high correlation between improvement in one function and improvement in other functions. While in every case there is a positive correlation, in no instance does this value rise sufficiently high to justify any definite statements of numerical values. While recognizing that these values are subject to a large attenuation correction, there is no doubt that under the conditions of these experiments there is no such function as high general improvability. All that we can say is that after correction for attenuation is made, there would probably be a small positive correlation between the improvements made in the various tests. In other words an individual who gained a definite amount in one test would show a slight tendency to gain to the same relative extent in the other tests.

One most important conclusion, however, results from these experiments in which the correlations between improvabilities have been measured. This is the extremely unsatisfactory nature of improvability over short periods, as a test or index of the individual, at least when the measurement of the improvement is in tests such as have been here used. It would appear from the variations in the values of Table XV, showing the correlations between the gains at two different periods in the practise curve, that this is one of the most uncertain measures which can be obtained. This uncertainty can be compared quantitatively with that of other measures. We have shown in the case of efficiencies as measured by product produced that there is a high correlation between the initial and final scores of each individual. No such high correlation is found in the case of improvabilities. If we make the following definitions:

initial improvement = sum (6+7+8) scores — sum (1+
    2+3) scores
final improvement = sum   (9+10) scores — sum   (4+5)
    scores

and then correlate these two measures, the numerical values shown in column 2 result. In column 3, for purposes of comparison, the correlations between

sum (9+10) and sum (1+2+3) are stated.

TABLE XVIII

CORRELATION BETWEEN EARLY AND LATE IMPROVEMENT

Column 2.   Gain (678–123) with gain (910–45).
Column 3.   Sum (1+2+3) with sum (9+10).

Test	Early and late improvement correlation	Early and late score correlation
Color...................	.19	.87
Cancellation 2..........	.35	.75
Cancellation 3..........	.31	.85
Opposites..............	.65	.59
Addition...............	.40	.96
Mental multiplication...	.48	.87

This table serves to show that, whereas there is a comparative regularity in the case of the gross scores at different periods of practise, when improvabilities are concerned there are great variations depending upon the actual period in the test at which the improvement is measured.   That is, if we arrange the subjects in relative order according to their power of gaining at the commencement of the test, there is no considerable maintenance of this relative order throughout the test.   If this is the case, measurements of improvements can have little significance unless they are conducted over very long periods of time.   It is possible that if we could select a few tests and allow each individual sufficient time to reach his limit, one of the best tests of the individual from the psychological and educational standpoint might result; but measurements of improvability extending over but a short period of time cannot give accurate results.   If any work is to be attempted, using improvability as the function to be measured, this present study indicates the practise will have to be of long duration, if any definite conclusions are to be reached.

The results apart from this study of the correlations between improvement are few.   Wimms ('07) states that after an examination of twelve boys of about 17 years of age, the correlation between improvability in addition and improvability in multiplication was .007.   Miss Race, in a research about to be published, has investigated the intercorrelation between improvements in three tests.   Two groups of college students of 28 and 31 individuals respectively were examined in addition, substitution and cancellation.   The period of practise in each case was 168 minutes, reckoning from the middle of the first test to the middle of the last test.   Miss Race has kindly supplied me with some preliminary values of the raw correlations calculated without allowance for errors in the scores. These values are shown below.

Correlation between improvements in tests	Group I	Group II
Additions and substitution..............	.47	.37
Addition and cancellation..............	.35	.55
Substitution and cancellation...........	.08	.18

At this point it may be well to mention in passing an important factor in the measurements of the correlations of improvabilities. It might appear that if there is a decided positive correlation between initial abilities, there would also be a corresponding correlation between powers of improvement; otherwise how can certain individuals have attained a generally superior position in all the tests, without the presence of a general power of improvement ? Certainly a decided positive correlation between improvements would result if we measured the progress from the time of infancy. However, much original nature may enter in determining efficiency; if we go back sufficiently in our measurements, we reach a point where in such tests as those used in this experiment there is no actual but only potential power. That is, if our measurements of improvement start with the untrained child, there must be present throughout a correlation between powers of improvement identical with those found in the direct correlations of present initial efficiencies, for in every case the initial score represents the gain from the supposed zero efficiency which is the actual power before training, as opposed to potential power. It is therefore necessary, when making determinations of improvement, to define with the greatest care at what point in the history of that particular trait in the individual life, this estimate is made.

Correlation Between Initial Efficiency and Improvement

The initial efficiency of any function as measured in these experiments represents that capacity which is present as a result of original nature and any specialized and general training which may have taken place prior to the time in question. The improvement made throughout the test period is a measure of the power of improvability quite apart from the absence or presence of initial training. A point of great interest arises as to the connection between initial ability and powers of improvement. Does the fact that an individual has already attained a relatively high efficiency in the function give a likelihood of a still further power of improvement, or is it true that this high efficiency has been gained at the expense of future progress? The answer to this question can be found by determining the correlations between initial score and improvement; as a measure of these we may accept the sum of the scores $(1+2+3)$ tests and the difference of scores $(6+7+8)$ tests—$(1+2+3)$ tests.

Whitley ('11) has shown the varying conclusions which arise from the treatment of the same data according as the gross or the percentile method is employed in measuring the improvement. The balance of favor certainly lies with the gross method, for only by this treatment can a clear idea be gained of the actual meaning of the results. Many anomalies arise when measurements are converted into percentage basis. For this reason the measurement of gain in this study is gross. The score $(6+7+8)$ —$(1+2+3)$ is perhaps a better estimate of the improvement than $(9+10)$—$(1+2)$ because the former is recorded before the final limit is reached in the case of the simpler tests. This entrance of the physiological limit vitiates comparison as it enables the individual who is slow in improvement to catch up to the fast individual, for the former gains while the latter is stationary. In spite of this, for purposes of comparison the score

$$\left[\frac{9+10}{2}\right] - \left[\frac{1+2+3}{3}\right]$$

is also taken as a measure of the improvement. Whatever score is used as the basis for calculating the gain, the arbitrary nature of the correlation obtained is indicated by the low correlations between initial and final improvements shown in Table XVIII, for these values indicate that between initial and final gain even in the same function there is no high inter-relation. Referring to Table XIX, the values of these correlations between initial ability and improvement admit of general explanation. In the case of the color test, the proximity to the physiological limit combined with the small amount of improvement which is possible would yield a low correlation. A similar reason holds with the opposites test. Here we have simply to assume that higher

TABLE XIX

CORRELATION BETWEEN INITIAL SCORES AND IMPROVEMENT

Column I. $\begin{aligned} Initial\ score &= (1+2+3) \\ Improvement &= (6+7+8) - (1+2+3) \end{aligned}$

Column II. $Improvement = \left[\frac{9+10}{2}\right] - \left[\frac{1+2+3}{3}\right]$

	Col. I Correlation	Col. II Correlation
Color	.03	—.14
Cancellation 2	.06	.05
Opposites	—.09	—.19
Addition	.44	.34
Multiplication	.28	.41

initial efficiency means that the function is nearer the end of the practise curve; under these conditions the gain of a given score is obviously much more difficult for the individual who has a higher initial efficiency. Again in the cancellation test, which is largely mechanical, the law of diminishing returns enters as it did in the case of the color and opposites test, producing a low correlation.

When we pass from the mechanical and association tests to those involving more complex functions, such as addition and mental multiplication, there is at once a decided rise in the correlations. In both these functions, high initial efficiency tends to be combined with a correspondingly greater power of improvement. This is largely due to the wider range of improvement which is possible in these more complex tests as opposed to the other more automatic tests. The difference between the range is shown in the practise curves. For an individual to have an initial high score in addition or mental multiplication does not imply that he is near his limit; in fact, he has before him in all probability a greater range of improvement than the person of low initial efficiency. The reverse is the case in the other mechanical functions,—the higher the initial score the nearer the individual is to his limit.

Improvement in the addition test has been measured by Thorndike ('10), Wells ('12), Kirby ('13), and others. Thorndike's results serve to show the relation between initial efficiency and improvement. The experiment consisted in adding daily for seven days forty-eight columns each of ten numbers. The time needed for this work and the errors made were recorded for each of nineteen subjects. When the scores are reduced to terms of single additions made with perfect accuracy, if we accept the score on the first day as representing initial efficiency and the gross gain from the first to the seventh day as the measure of the gain, there is an evident correlation between high initial efficiency and power of improvement. This positive value of the correlation is also supported by Wells's experiments to which reference has already been made. According to an examination of these curves high initial scoring in no way precludes, but on the other hand frequently indicates, the expectation of considerable practise improvement. He concludes: "We are evidently confronted with cases indicating a high initial efficiency as a manifestation of superior ability to profit by practise, and on the other hand with cases exhibiting a lower initial efficiency with minor possibilities of practise improvement." In an elaborate study Kirby tested a large number of school children in addition, having each of the classes practise adding these columns for 75 minutes. A curve plotted showing the relation between initial ability and improvement indicates once more that with high initial ability a correspondingly greater amount of improvement may be expected.

In the case of mental multiplication the results reached in this study are in fair agreement with those obtained by Whitley ('11) who had nine subjects do three-place by three-place examples such as those described. If allowance is made for the differences in the practise period, it is found that the four who were most efficient at the start made a greater average gain than the four who were least efficient. I have worked out the correlation between initial efficiencies and gross gain as given by Starch ('11), who found with eight subjects the improvement in mental multiplication of a three-place by a one-place number over a period of 14 days, in which ten minutes per day was spent in practise. This correlation is .22, which corresponds to the value .35 of this study. In Thorndike's ('08) experiment with 28 individuals, tested in mental multiplication while doing 95 examples, although the times spent in practise are of unequal lengths, there is, after allowing for this, a distinct positive correlation between initial efficiency and gross gain. He concludes "that in this experiment the larger individual differences increase with equal training, showing a positive correlation of high initial ability with ability to profit by practise."

In the unpublished study of improvement by Miss Race, which has been previously mentioned, the correlations between initial scores and improvement with no allowance for error have been calculated in the case of the three tests used. The results are shown:

Addition...............	.38
Substitution...........	—.25
Cancellation...........	—.08

Here again, there is a considerable correlation between initial ability and improvement in addition, while negative correlations are found in the substitution and cancellation tests.

To summarise, it appears that in complex functions an individual who has gained high efficiency by previous general training will also improve correspondingly during the practise period; whereas in narrow functions, as usually scored, initial efficiency probably bears little relation to improvability. If the method of scoring was altered so as to weight improvement which is made as the subject approaches the physiological limit, there is little doubt that high correlations would be obtained in the narrow functions.

These conclusions, if they are justified by further experiments, are of great educational importance. It might be supposed that the individual who has already attained considerable standing in a subject is in a better position to improve by further training; such a result as this would naturally be expected in purely informational subjects. What is much less obvious and hardly to be expected is that the same principle of increasing returns should operate in such a comparatively simple test as addition or mental multiplication. It affords support, based on actual measurements, to the old truism, "to him that hath shall be given," upon which the selective process of education is based.

Correlation Between Efficiency and Accuracy

The relation between efficiency and accuracy will be treated in the briefest manner, for only in three of the tests can estimates be made of the extent of the errors. The method of scoring the multiplication test is too arbitrary to justify its inclusion.

For the purpose of these correlations we may define efficiency in the tests as measured by the total product produced after allowance has been made for errors on the basis mentioned when the tests were described. In this manner we are not estimating efficiency by quantity of work irrespective of error but rather by product which is up to a certain level of attainment. The accuracy is measured by finding the number of errors made by the subject when producing a score of 100 units. In ranking the individuals in efficiency and accuracy the first place is given to the lowest total scorer and the least accurate individual respectively, so that a positive correlation indicates that efficiency (speed) is accompanied by accuracy. The following values result:

TABLE XX

CORRELATION BETWEEN EFFICIENCY AND ACCURACY

Measures.   Efficiency = total correct product produced in all the tests.
Accuracy = errors made per 100 of corrected score.

In determining Spearman Coefficient, the least efficient and the least accurate subjects are ranked one in each case.

Test	Correlation between efficiency and accuracy
Cancellation 2	+.05
Cancellation 3	—.13
Addition	.62

It should be noticed in the determination of these coefficients that each figure which contributes is the result of ten individual measurements.

The difference between the relationship between efficiency and accuracy in the cancellation tests and the addition test can be explained. In the latter function, the reason for the high efficiency of an individual is due to the fact that he has found in his previous work sufficient accuracy to justify greater speed; in other words, the controlling factor as regards speed, over the whole of the previous training, has been the accuracy attained. We should therefore expect that high speed would be the accompaniment of a low percentage error.

In the case of the cancellation tests there has been no time, owing to lack of training in the function, for this adjustment of speed and accuracy to take place. On this account little correlation between efficiency and accuracy is to be looked for.

The high value obtained in the addition test indicates that in functions where sufficient time has elapsed for equilibrium between speed and accuracy to be established there is a decided tendency for the fast worker to be also the most accurate.

Summary

In this study, twenty-two individuals have been examined in the following tests: color naming, cancellation, opposites, addition and mental multiplication. Each individual was tested on ten occasions. In this way a measure is obtained of initial efficiency and improvability.

The practise curves of a random sampling of individuals have been examined for each test. In addition, composite practise curves for the twenty-two individuals have been drawn.

The following intercorrelations in the tests have been determined:

(1) Initial ability with initial ability
(2) Improvability with improvability
(3) Initial ability with final ability
(4) Initial ability with improvability
(5) Efficiency with accuracy

Conclusions

The composite practise curves reveal by their difference in form the various rates of improvement which take place in the functions measured. In simple tests, such as color naming and opposites, which rapidly become automatic, the curves show that an approach is made to the psychological limit even in such short amounts of practise as fifteen minutes. The more complex tests require a much greater time; the curves for addition and mental multiplication indicate that even after practise of 100 and 200 minutes respectively, improvement is still almost as rapid as at the commencement, especially in the somewhat difficult mental multiplication.

The individual practise curves have been used for the purpose of investigating the nature of the cause which accounts for the variability in the individual scores when measured at different times. Is the decrease in efficiency exhibited in one test of sufficient duration and general influence to operate in the same test or other tests when applied within a few minutes ?   In the case of the individual curves for the cancellation 2 and cancellation 3 tests, performed within one half minute of each other, there is no obvious relation between a decrease in efficiency in the one test, and a decrease in efficiency in the other test.   We are therefore bound to conclude that the subjective conditions which affect the score, unless very severe, are of such short duration as not to operate over a period as short as three minutes.

The correlations between initial abilities in each of the tests are positive, varying between .2 and .3 as an average.   These values are lower than those found in previous studies.   The reasons for this lowness are discussed.   The values are sufficiently uniform to indicate that there exists to a small extent, over the range of tests used, a power corresponding to general intelligence or efficiency.

The intercorrelations between improvements in the tests are found to be slight but of a positive order.   When it is considered that the improvements are measured over such short times and at different points in the complete practise curve of the function starting from infancy, this low correlation is explained. These coefficients would rise in value the earlier in the life of the individual the measurement of the initial score was made, reaching the limit when the initial scores represent zero ability, for under these conditions the correlations between improvements become identical with those between initial scores.

The main contribution of this investigation of improvabilities is to reveal the complete inadequacy of measurements of improvement over short periods as a test of individual differences.

The maintenance of rank of each individual throughout any particular test is evidenced by the very high correlation between the initial and final scores.

In the more complex tests, such as addition and mental multiplication, high initial efficiency seems to be accompanied by a correspondingly great power of improvement.   No such power of improvement shows itself in the case of the more automatic tests.

In the case of a much practised function, such as addition, it appears that high efficiency tends to be accompanied by a corresponding accuracy.   The cancellation tests, in which there has been no previous training, fail to reveal any close relationship.

BIBLIOGRAPHY

BROWN (09). Some Experimental Results in the Correlation of Mental Abilities. *Brit. Jour. Psych.*, Vol. 3, p. 296.

BURT (09). Experimental Tests of General Intelligence. *Brit. Jour. Psych.*, Vol. 3, p. 94.

HOLLINGWORTH (12). Influence of Cafein on Mental and Motor Efficiency. Columbia Univ. Archives of Psychology, No. 22.

HOLLINGWORTH (13). Correlation of Abilities as Affected by Practice. *Jour. Educ. Psych.*, Sept., 1913.

KIRBY (13). Practise in the Case of School Children. Teachers College, Columbia Univ., Contributions to Education, No. 58.

SIMPSON (12). Correlation of Mental Abilities. Teachers College, Columbia Univ., Contributions to Education, No. 53.

SPEARMAN (04). General Intelligence Objectively Determined and Measured. *Amer. Jour. Psych.*, Vol. 15, p. 201.

SPEARMAN and KRUEGER (06). Die Korrelation zwischen verschiedenen geistigen Leistungsfahigkeiten. *Zeitschrift fur Psychologie*, Bd. 19, s. 50.

STARCH (11). Transfer of Training in Arithmetical Operations. *Jour. Educ. Psych.*, Vol. 2, p. 306.

THORNDIKE (08). Effect of Practise in the Case of a Purely Intellectual Function. *Amer. Jour. Psych.*, Vol. 19, p. 374.

THORNDIKE (09). Relation of Accuracy in Sensory Discrimination to General Intelligence. *Amer. Jour. Psych.*, Vol. 20, p. 364.

THORNDIKE (10). Practise in the Case of Addition. *Amer. Jour. Psych.*, Vol. 21, p. 483.

WELLS (12). The Relation of Practise to Individual Differences. *Amer. Jour. Psych.*, Vol. 23, p. 75.

WIMMS (07). The Relative Effects of Fatigue and Practice Produced by Different Kinds of Mental Work. *Brit. Jour. Psych.*, Vol. 2, p. 153.

WHITLEY (11). An Empirical Study of Certain Tests for Individual Differences. Columbia Univ. Archives of Psychology, No. 19.

WOODWORTH AND WELLS (11). Association Tests. Psychological Monographs, No. 57.